Bible

**7 Sessions for Homegroup
and Personal Use**

The
Sermon
on the *Mount*

Life within the new covenant

Chris Leonard

Contents

Introduction

'What about war then, God?' 'This world You say is Yours – what about suffering, oppression, injustice, the breakdown of relationships?' 'Some of us are worried sick. If You're in charge, what's the deal? What do You want?' 'Can You help us? If so, how on earth should we relate to You, communicate with You?'

Good questions. Surf the radio channels and you'll hear them over and over again in rock music, discussions, comedy, documentaries … 'If you're in charge, what's the deal?' is exactly what Jesus explains in the Sermon on the Mount.

People were asking similar questions when Jesus started His work in Galilee, only more urgently. Most of God's 'Chosen People' then were living well below the breadline, under brutal Roman occupation, hoping against hope that God would rescue them. John the Baptist had prepared the way for One who would comfort, rescue, restore His people following a lengthy period of God's judgment and silence (see Isa. 40, Matt. 3). Matthew parallels Jesus with Moses. Both arrive in Egypt. Both escape the wholesale slaughter of fellow-infants, spend time in the wilderness, then perform miracles (in Jesus' case, of healing and deliverance) to set people free. Each climbs a mountain. That's where Jesus delivers the Sermon – intense teaching signalling new developments in a story reaching back into pre-history, and forward … for as long as this world lasts.

God had made deals (covenants) with Israel through Abraham, David and others – notably through Moses on Mount Sinai. Jesus made all of these new, literally fleshing out the covenant deal with Israel through His Sermon – and His life. But a covenant requires the agreement of two or more parties. Jewish civic and religious authorities rejected Jesus and His covenant. The story doesn't end there, though. A covenant deal was always sealed by a blood sacrifice. When the Jewish religious authorities, opposing God's new deal, had the Romans crucify Jesus, the irony was that they made Him the sacrifice. That ratified the deal for anyone, of any race, who chose to take it up.

But what about those urgent, even accusatory questions with which we started? The Sermon's covenant deal answers them all. The answers aren't easy, because they involve us. Us working in partnership with God. A covenant deal, like a marriage agreement, defines the relationship between two (or more) parties, the way they behave towards each other and the rest. Normally one party would be the top dog, the lord, the king (and that's not us!). The lord sets the terms, normally promising benefits and blessings if they are kept, sanctions and curses if not.

Jesus came to say that God still wants to relate to people, even though we have messed up the relationship again and again. Beginning His Sermon with blessings (and in Luke's parallel passage, with curses too) Jesus' idea of happiness and blessing turned – still turns – expectations upside down. How could poor, gentle, persecuted mourners be described as 'happy' or 'blessed'?

Suddenly, instead of hurling question-accusations at God, we find ourselves asking, 'What kind of people does God want? Which attitudes impress, or sadden, Him? How might that affect our behaviour, our priorities? How can we, this time, build relationships with God and human beings on ground that won't break up under our feet?'

In Matthew's Gospel, Jesus is very much a king, ruling and reigning very differently from others as He ushers in the kingdom of heaven on earth. That kingdom, revealed in His Sermon, parables, miracles, life, death and resurrection, is not fully come, even yet, but the Sermon on the Mount describes the deal for its citizens. It's the same deal God has always wanted for all people on His earth: to be like Him, to be holy as He is holy. This deal, this passionate desire of God, has nothing to do with religion, with ascetic monk-like separation from the world or even with warm, spiritual feelings. It has everything to do with relationships, on His terms, with Himself, with the world He created and with the people He loves – which is everyone. It has everything to do with our learning to depend on Him as in His Name we confront suffering, oppression, violence, injustice, the breakdown of relationships … everything which spoils His wonderful world.

Jesus' words in this Sermon still have power to shock – partly because we can't push them into some corner of mere outward conformity. They describe a complete and utter change from within, which then changes the world. The Sermon challenges the Christian Church about straying from the deal today as much as it did the former worshippers at the Jewish Temple. We're saved – included in the benefits of the new covenant – by God's grace. We grow within His covenant, His kingship, by His grace – but only if we co-operate in that growth. He doesn't bludgeon us. His kingship is not expressed through domination but through empowering others, through love, through sacrifice. Ultimately, the deal equips us to reign with Him.

So, expect plenty of challenges as you do this study. But remember that the Sermon isn't the whole story. The sacrifice of Jesus cleanses and heals us, His resurrection life empowers us and His Holy Spirit lives closer than our breath, to lead us into all truth.

WEEK 1

Renewed Deal

Opening Icebreaker and Worship

Think of an agreement you've entered into. Share one privilege and one responsibility it has brought.

Do the same for your agreement to follow Jesus. Express it in prayers of thankfulness. And/or share bread and wine together, celebrating the new covenant made in His blood.

Bible Readings

- Genesis 1:26–31
- Exodus 19:3–8
- Matthew 4:12–5:2
- Deuteronomy 30:11–20
- Matthew 26:18–30
- Hebrews 12:18–24

Opening Our Eyes

I find the three chapters of Matthew's Gospel which
make up the Sermon on the Mount the most difficult in
the whole Bible. It's not that they are especially hard to
understand, but they are Jesus' own words, so we need to
pay the closest attention. His new covenant is so central
to His teaching, to who He is, to what He expects from
us. The Sermon is teaching – packed dense, difficult
teaching. Full of opposites held in tension, one minute it
seems impossibly harsh, the next full of extravagant love
and grace. I find it more than challenging. My thoughts
and reason, my imagination, let alone my relationships
and actions, get left way behind.

Yet Jesus' teaching, thought, reason, imagination,
relationships and actions never were shockingly new.
They go right back to what God always intended. That's
why we're beginning the story at the very beginning,
before rebelliousness corrupted people's relationships
with God and with one another.

The core of any story centres around relationships
– and that includes who's boss. Shortly after creating
human beings, God delegated authority over part of His
earth to them (Gen. 1:26–31). Much of the Bible's story
shows how events and relationships depend on the way
authority is exercised. God's way is to renew, empower,
liberate and draw closer. The human way has often
been to belittle, abuse, enslave and alienate. The 'big
story' of the Bible tells of God's initiatives to restore right
authority, whether His own or delegated. Godly authority
enables people to become free and whole, empowered
for good, loved and loving, protecting the weak, working
with Him for peace and justice. That's what His kingdom
is – the kingdom we pray will 'come on earth as it is in
heaven'. In Adam's, Moses', Joshua's, David's and Jesus'
day people were slow to learn. They needed guidelines,

agreements. We're the same, though we have more help through the graces of the cross, the resurrection and the ever-present Holy Spirit. Jesus' Sermon gives us a healthy reminder of what the deal requires – and how very much we depend on God's grace in order to fulfil those requirements.

The angels proclaimed peace on earth at Jesus' birth. We look around and don't see much peace. Evidently we need to change if we're to see more of His kingdom come in our own lives, let alone globally.

It's good, on the other hand, to remind ourselves of how the world has changed for the better as a result of this new deal which Jesus brought. It's taken a while, but in most countries where Christian influence has been brought to bear, slavery is abolished, government may irritate but isn't despotic, justice no longer demands 'an eye for an eye', women can't be made destitute just because their husband says 'I divorce you' three times. Authority is at least trying to be seen as doing good.

So, before tackling these three difficult chapters in any depth, spend some time examining and grounding yourself in the big picture – first in the Bible and then in your own life and in the complex, part-godly, part-fallen world in which we all live. In His Sermon, Jesus invites us to imagine the deal from His point of view. The extent to which we imagine, and then live in, the world that way, will be the extent to which we'll see miracles of poor, gentle, persecuted mourners becoming happy – the extent to which we'll see His Sermon becoming reality.

Discussion Starters

1. Genesis 1:26–31. In what ways has human authority become corrupted, veering from God's intention and from the way He Himself would rule?

2. Exodus 19:4–5. What were the privileges and responsibilities offered to Israel under the Mosaic covenant?

3. Did they have a wider mission on earth than keeping their own people holy?

4. Exodus 19:3–8. Before Moses asked the people whether they wanted to enter into the covenant with God, they had already received much blessing and freedom. How is similar grace demonstrated in Matthew 4:12–5:2?

5. Could that affect the way we share the good news?

6. What can you learn from Matthew 4:12–5:2 of God's big story, of the people called to follow Jesus and of the good news He brought before preaching His Sermon?

_____

_____

7. Deuteronomy 30:11–20. What strength and encouragement do you find here?

_____

_____

8. Give examples of how following God's commands and Jesus' teaching brings life rather than death, blessings rather than curses?

_____

_____

9. Matthew 26:18–30. Explore what 'This is my blood of the [new] covenant' means – and how you might embrace that aspect of grace when you next remember Jesus' death.

_____

_____

10. Hebrews 12:18–24. What encouragement can you draw from this – especially anything that might help when you start looking at the Sermon on the Mount?

_____

_____

Personal Application

Entering into the new covenant, means accepting the new deal – that God is boss. He uses (and delegates) His authority in ways which, to our corrupted mind-sets, can seem strange. So maybe this is time for a reality check. How and when is God really your boss? And when isn't He? How far are you dependent on Him? Especially when it comes to following Jesus? Where and to whom has He delegated you authority? At work? In your family? In your community? Are you using that authority in a way which empowers others to love? Are you learning in small ways to rule as He would rule?

Seeing Jesus in the Scriptures

'Now when he saw the crowds, [Jesus] went up on a mountainside and sat down. His disciples came to him, and he began to teach them' (Matt. 5:1–2). Jesus got up close and personal for His Sermon, teaching first the ones who had given up everything to follow Him. He sat down (then a sign of a teacher's authority). Just as disciples sat at the feet of any rabbi, the disciples would have sat at His feet. As we study the Sermon on the Mount, let us do the same, remembering also that, 'Since, then, you have been raised with Christ, set your hearts on things above, where Christ is seated at the right hand of God. Set your minds on things above, not on earthly things' (Col. 3:1–2). We'll never get there by our own efforts, so let's fix our eyes on Him, His strength, His grace, His authority.

WEEK 2

Renewed People

Opening Icebreaker and Worship

Give one example of someone you know who is truly happy – and say why you think this is so.

Worship God, the great I AM – and Jesus, who said, 'I am the way, the truth and the life.'

Bible Readings

- Matthew 5:3–12, 13–16
- 1 Peter 1:13–25
- Luke 6:20–26
- Deuteronomy 30
- Psalm 1

Opening Our Eyes

The contract for this (or any) book begins by defining, in careful, legal language, exactly who the parties are: the identity of author and publisher and the relationship between them. The structure of the new covenant isn't that different. Jesus, by word and action, made clear who He was before, and after, preaching the Sermon on the Mount. John's Gospel reports Jesus' seven 'I am' sayings (vine, light, water ...). God told Moses His name: 'I AM'. The whole Bible reveals His character, who He is.

But, if He is 'I AM', what about 'you are'? First: it's a plural 'you'. This covenant defines a relationship with a people, so it's about how we get on with each other as well as with God. Second: you (or we) are ... *not* the same people as those who entered into the old covenant. We're a bunch of rejects.

The first part of Jesus' Sermon defines who we are, not by nationality or ancestry as the old contract did. Jesus' definitions must have shocked His audience – especially the learned ones who'd thought they understood. Probably the children 'got it' best. Our minister told us how his son complained that a boy kept inviting everyone to join a game of football at junior school lunch-time, only to tell various individuals that, for assorted random reasons, they couldn't play. 'Dad, can I take a football to school? I want to start a game for all the disqualified people.'

That was a profoundly 'new covenant' thing to do. Once disqualified rejects, we've become essential salt and light for others – and are happy. The word means exactly that – 'fortunate', 'winners' or 'to be congratulated' rather than 'religiously blessed'.

In nine short verses, Jesus stretches our imagination – saying happy people are, of all things, poor, mourning, gentle, hungry, merciful, single-minded, persecuted peacemakers. We'll unpack those 'beautiful attitudes' more later. They have to do with the centrality of our relationship with Him, our becoming utterly dependent and increasingly like Him in character. (Radical and mind-blowing – 'being holy as He is holy' was also central to Moses' covenant.)

In the late 1980s some Chinese Christians, who had suffered for years in prison because of their faith, were released. On being asked what they thought of foreign Christians, they said that the Westerners knew much about God, while they, who had been starved of Bibles, teaching, corporate worship, pastoral care and fellowship, knew God Himself. You could say these Chinese saints were 'winners' – as well as mourning, poor, persecuted and all the rest. That helps me understand – a quiet life or easy contentment isn't for those whom Jesus called 'happy'. Those Chinese, loving God, yearned only for the same thing as He did. Neither they nor He have yet found it because His kingdom, the way He wants the world to work, hasn't fully come. Too many (unlike those described in the 'deal') show ugly attitudes – spiritual arrogance, aggression, lack of compassion, apathy, unrighteousness, ruthlessness, double-mindedness. Some persecute God's people. If you, like me, feel like pleading 'guilty as charged' – well, that throws us on God. Jesus' sacrifice has dealt with our guilt so, though everything promised in the 'contract' isn't fully worked out yet, we can keep walking boldly towards Him, becoming a little more like Him, being salt and light for others.

Beyond happiness, the deal is being equipped for the future, to reign with Christ when His kingdom does come. No more tears when all will have found mercy and see God.

Discussion Starters

1. What difference does it make to think of relationship with God primarily as 'with me as an individual' or 'with us'? Which occurs more in the Bible?

2. What does it mean to be 'poor in spirit' etc?

3. Which of Jesus' examples of what it means to be happy most surprises you?

4. List the opposite qualities. What would happen if everyone was like that?

5. How do the future promises or consequences (eg inheriting the earth) relate to each Beatitude? What about the opposite consequences, eg if you're not merciful, what happens?

6. What do the Beatitudes tell us about God's character – and of the kind of authority He exercises and desires in us?

_____

_____

7. How does Matthew 5:3–16 ignite our imaginations and show us how we might begin to become holy as He is holy? (Read 1 Peter 1:13–25)

_____

_____

8. Matthew 5:13–16 urges the new, holy people to 'infect' the world with God's distinctive goodness. How does the distinctiveness which springs from your relationship with God make a difference in your community or workplace?

_____

_____

9. Luke 6:20–26. Like penalty and reward clauses in contracts, blessings and cursings normally accompanied ancient covenants. They do in Luke's parallel passage. Read this and Deuteronomy 30 in the light of the 'narrow path' later in Jesus' sermon (Matt. 7:13–14). What consequences of reneging on 'the deal' have you observed?

_____

_____

10. How might Psalm 1 help your understanding of the Beatitudes?

_____

_____

Personal Application

Draw closer to God. This 'deal' is all about relationship and we're not going to fulfil our part of it unless He lives His life through us. More than doing, this is about being. Being with Him. Being as He would be as we go about our daily lives. Maybe a good question to ask is 'Where is whatever we most value?' or 'Where is our treasure?' as Jesus said. In God? Also in the people He created and loves? If so, we'll enjoy heaven – and work to bring the kingdom of heaven on earth. Worship means giving worth to God not just in song or prayer but in the whole of our lives, being the people He wants us to be!

Seeing Jesus in the Scriptures

Jesus never asks us to do or be something which He is not. He emptied Himself to become poor in spirit as well as materially poor and vulnerable. He wept over Jerusalem. He was gentle, made God's will His food and drink, was merciful, single-minded, especially in setting His face to go to Jerusalem when He knew it would mean crucifixion. He, the Prince of Peace, was persecuted for most of His ministry as well as through His death. He was light (see Matt. 4:15–16). He was salt – astringent, disinfecting, preserving, bringing out all the flavours God intended. He was also happy – anointed with 'the oil of joy' above His companions (Heb. 1:9). And He and the Father are so close that They are one.

WEEK 3

Renewed Morality

Opening Icebreaker and Worship

Give one example from the past week when your relationship with God influenced a moral decision you took.

Worship God in His goodness.

Bible Readings

- Matthew 5:17–37
- 2 Corinthians 5:14–21
- Philippians 3:4–21
- Hebrews 8:8–12
- Malachi 2:14–17

Opening Our Eyes

Jesus said, 'Unless your righteousness surpasses that of the Pharisees and the teachers of the law, you will certainly not enter the kingdom of heaven' (Matt. 5:20). That sounds like bad news. We might as well pack up and go home! Except that, in covenants, the parties swap things – goods as part of the deal or their coats perhaps, as a sign of the deal. Originally, it seems, a third person mingled the two parties' blood – blood which stood for someone's life. We swap too. We get Jesus' righteousness: He gets our sin. We get His life: He gets what we deserve – death. 'God made him who had no sin to be sin for us, so that in him we might become the righteousness of God' (2 Cor. 5:21).

St Paul, himself a Pharisee, considered his own religious efforts at righteousness rubbish, 'Not having a righteousness of my own that comes from the law, but that which is through faith in Christ – the righteousness that comes from God and is by faith' (Phil. 3:8–9).

Jesus was the only man ever to fulfil the Law truly. He understood it was, like God's very nature, rooted in relationships – its purpose to make human/divine and human relationships better. For example, He said, 'The Sabbath was made for man, not man for the Sabbath' (Mark 2:27–28). Workers, mothers, leaders – everyone needs time to rest from work, special time to enjoy God and one another.

Jesus fulfilled all the sacrificial laws, ending them once and for all. But, far from abolishing the moral Law, He deepened and renewed it. How people relate to one another matters to God. Also, for any kingdom to work, its citizens need agreed behavioural principles. In Matthew 5:17–37 Jesus homes in on three fundamental sins which, almost from the very beginning, have disrupted community. The first lie recorded in the Bible takes place as early as Genesis 3. The next chapter sees murder and adultery (actually, polygamy which still flies in the face of the 'one flesh' of Genesis 2:24). Moses' covenant lays out punishments for its lawbreakers – but this is not our covenant. Jesus' death fulfils the Law's judicial aspects under His new covenant. There are still consequences though, if we treat people badly. For example, for some of his teenage years our son told us lies which he swore blind were the truth. The consequent breakdown in trust within our family relationships made living in the same house painful and difficult.

Suppose our bad motivations could be changed so that the offences never happened, wouldn't life and relationships go far better, for God and for people? We need God's help far more over our inner thought-life, our attitudes and motivations than our actions. Only He may see our bouts of brooding anger and unforgiveness, or the extent to which our sexual fantasies stray outside of marriage. Only He knows when we're not absolutely straight in what we say or promise. Our inner attitudes affect the way we're facing – and thus the direction we're likely to take. Are we moving towards God, towards love? Or towards impulses which come from somewhere else – selfishness, our own inner damage, even evil?

Don't give up and go home – Jesus' teaching is ultimately liberating. Remember the promise in Hebrews 8:10, 'This is the covenant I will make … declares the Lord. I will put my laws in their minds and write them on their hearts. I will be their God, and they will be my people.'

Discussion Starters

1. Do you see God's Law in a positive or a negative light?

2. Has the Holy Spirit written it in your mind and heart or do you strain to obey rules?

3. Do you obey Leviticus 19:19 and 27 'Do not wear clothing woven of two kinds of material' and 'Do not cut the hair at the sides of your head or clip off the edges of your beard'? Why not?

4. How does the 'swapping' of your own sinful bias for Jesus' righteousness work in thought and attitude as well as action?

5. How can you help one another stir up faith for the righteousness that comes from God?

6. What, in your opinion, most damages relationships within a community – murder, adultery, divorce, lying … or something else? Why?

_____

_____

7. How does the way God feels about all people affect the way you relate to others – particularly in the light of practical instructions given in Matthew 5:21–26?

_____

_____

8. What helpful and godly ways have you found of dealing with conflict?

_____

_____

9. As a form of covenant-breaking (see Mal. 2:14–17), is divorce an unforgivable sin? How would God want us to treat people who are divorced and remarried?

_____

_____

10. Matthew 5:33–37. Confession time! What has driven you to lie and what were the consequences?

_____

_____

Personal Application

This is about as close and personal as it gets. None of us feel comfortable when challenged about our attitudes – especially those which involve anger, sex, divorce, or lies. We may try to pretend these things don't touch us – but they do. And this is not only about personal morality. Each one of these things affects other people. Each one leads to a form of control.

Remember, the deal is that God's in control, so these issues should never be out of bounds, even in a nice, respectable church setting. If we suppress, rather than confess and get God's help to deal with them, we'll end up with something far worse. Suppressed anger leads to depression. Families can pay hell when domestic violence is hidden to 'preserve marriage'. Suppressed sexuality can lead to all kinds of deviant behaviour. On the other hand, if no family were stable, if everyone lied, or followed up each sexual desire and angry thought, society would collapse.

Seeing Jesus in the Scriptures

Jesus seems at His harshest in passages like this – and of course He always has deep concerns about the way we treat each other. But we need to see His words here in the context of His whole life and death – His actions and reactions. Think about the way He accepted people who had been involved in lies or adultery. Follow Him in the way you treat others. Now that you've read His words, let His words read you. Let His truth and His Spirit set you free.

WEEK 4

Renewed Justice

Opening Icebreaker and Worship

Which injustice, large or small, bugs you most?

Read Isaiah 42:1–7 and Philippians 2:6–11. Worship Jesus.

Bible Readings

- Matthew 5:38–44; 7:1–6
- Luke 6:27–38,41,42; 10:25–37
- Romans 12:9–21
- Isaiah 42:1–7

Opening Our Eyes

But God, what about the evil in Your world? You're just. What's the deal?

Justice – including what to do about the consequences of evil and people or organisations caught up in it – echoes throughout the Old Testament. The word, also translated 'righteousness', is central to God's nature and to what He requires of us. According to Micah 6:8 that is, 'To act justly and to love mercy and to walk humbly with your God.' Mercy means loving-kindness – another central characteristic of God which sits alongside His justice/righteousness as we engage in a close, dependent relationship with Him and the people He loves. Our 'neighbour', in the masterfully condensed two commandments of Jesus' new deal (Luke 10:25–37), isn't necessarily someone we like or feel comfortable with. God also created, and loves, those who became His enemies and ours.

Justice leapt forward under Moses' covenant, limiting vendettas to 'like for like' damage – 'an eye for an eye'. Jesus said, 'Love your enemies.' And did it, too. By rights, vengeance is God's – but He's not wiped humankind out as we deserve. In Him, justice and mercy meet. His punishments aren't for retribution but to bring about restoration – that we might move towards becoming perfect as He is perfect. He wants us to share His concept of justice, of generosity – to further those values on earth rather than being caught up in our personal grievances. His grace cuts both ways. He's asking us to treat others as we'd hope He (and they) would treat us.

Walter Wink's book *The Powers That Be* helped deepen my understanding of this passage. He believes that all organisations – churches, companies, nations – have their own character, which becomes corrupt once diverted from its original, God-given mission. God, often through His people, is recalling these corrupted 'powers' to their original purpose. His is the true power, authority and glory. We're not to resist the usurping powers using their own methods – violence and coercion. God has other ways.

So, if a Roman soldier exercised his right, as they did all the time, to command you to carry his pack for a mile, you didn't refuse, you carried it two. He had strict orders not to demand that. Your kindness might make him think, or even get him into trouble! If a right-handed person struck you on the right cheek it would be with the back of his hand – the kind of blow offered to an inferior – a slave or woman. By offering your left cheek instead you'd imply, 'If you're going to hit me, do it as an equal.' If you were in debt and the court awarded the lender your tunic, you'd have no clothes left but your coat. Your nakedness on giving that too would shame him. Jesus isn't suggesting any of these examples is *the* way to resist injustice. He is encouraging innovative, non-coercive ways. For example, at their trial, a group of women opposing American nuclear capability in England kept responding to barristers' questions by singing choruses from Gilbert and Sullivan operettas. Their comic absurdity demanded, 'Where is the justice here?'

It sounds simple, if 'upside down', to oppose evil, not with more evil, but with good. But does it work? People haven't often tried but, where they have, it seems to. Gandhi, though a Hindu, followed Jesus' teaching in this. He led non-violent resistance that ended the British Empire's rule of India. Wink's book gives many other instances, large and small, which have worked, warning that they take enormous courage.

Discussion Starters

1. When you feel you've no control over a situation in which some injustice is being perpetrated, how do you react?

_____

_____

2. How might that change if you're conscious that God is in control?

_____

_____

3. In what sense might He be in control?

_____

_____

4. Jesus turned (and still does turn) our human attitudes and responses upside down. If you heard Him preach the words in Matthew 5:38–44 today, what question would you ask Him?

_____

_____

_____

5. The parallel passage in Luke exhorts us to imitate God's generosity. Can you give examples from your own experience of human relationships where generosity and/or mercy have proved more fruitful than retribution?

_____

_____

_____

6. How – and in what sense – did Jesus 'bring justice to the nations' (Isa. 42:1–7)?

_____

_____

_____

7. How can we follow Him in this?

_____

_____

_____

8. Romans 12:14–21. What non-violent, non-coercive strategies has God given you to resist evil?

_____

_____

_____

9. When have you overcome evil with good?

_____

_____

_____

10. Luke 10:25–37. How can we love our enemies – in heart, word and action?

_____

_____

_____

Personal Application

'Love', in English, can sound comforting, sentimental and non-moral – I love chocolate, a friend, England … But the particular kind of love Jesus demands in this passage (from the Greek word *agape*) is tough – as tough as the cross.

Some of us may appease what we dislike, the bullying individuals or organisations that unfairly cause us grief. Jesus isn't asking for appeasement. He's asking us to find ways to right wrongs by blessing (thus possibly wrong-footing) wrongdoers. Do we trust God for the courage to do this? Can we believe that this is the way He would chose to turn such a person or organisation back to His good purposes? Church history shows not all Christians have taken Him at His word. Can we?

Seeing Jesus in the Scriptures

Jesus said, 'I did not come to judge the world, but to save it' (John 12:47) then warns of judgment for those who reject Him and His words. Look again at Isaiah's passage foretelling Jesus' ministry. Jesus' words matched His actions and God-given mission every time. Glorious because He holds grace and truth together, at huge cost to Himself, His love looses restorative justice on a rebellious world – if only they'll receive.

'The Word became flesh and made his dwelling among us. We have seen his glory … full of grace and truth … From the fulness of his grace we have all received one blessing after another. For the law was given through Moses; grace and truth came through Jesus Christ' (John 1:14–17).

WEEK 5

Renewed God-conversations

Opening Icebreaker and Worship

What is the oddest prayer you've ever heard?

Read Psalm 100, then use the phrase, 'Our Father in heaven, hallowed be your name' as a basis for worship.

Bible Readings

- Matthew 6:1–18 and 7:7–11
- Luke 11:1–13
- Exodus 20:2–7
- 1 Chronicles 29:10–20
- Isaiah 58
- Malachi 2:10–3:1

Opening Our Eyes

No relationships exist without some form of conversation. Prayer, of course, is conversation with God. So is fasting – it's saying, 'Your word is more important to me than food.' Forgiveness, too. Jesus has strong words, even within 'The Lord's Prayer', about the essential connection between forgiveness and God-conversation. But have you ever thought of giving as conversation with God? It doesn't have to be. Its purpose can be demonstrating to other people what a wonderful Christian you are – which is something altogether different. Central to everything Jesus says in this part of His Sermon is the question: are we really wanting to further our relationship with God, or concerned more with impressing people?

Moses' covenant had plenty to say about worship. And worship, in its fullest sense, is what this section of Jesus' Sermon explores, because worship is about more than sacrifice, singing, or even praying. It's about our love-relationship with God. It's about declaring our love through our words and lives that He's worth everything to us.

Moses' covenant comes from a 'jealous' God who wants the best for His people – and that includes their wholehearted affection. Righteousness and jealousy can belong together. I was once with my husband and two other Christian married couples when the wife of one focused five hours of her attention on trying to impress the husband of the other. He appeared friendly but unmoved by her. John and I, definitely unimpressed by her antics, became too concerned to leave them to it. During that long, uncomfortable evening you could say we were jealous – not of anyone, but *for* their respective partners – and, yes, for righteousness, for God.

This session we're considering God-conversations. Think about holding a conversation with your friends or your boss. What words do you use? Many? Few? When and why is your speech restrained? When you're nervous, do you say more, or less? How do you react when the other person is quiet, or silent? What part does action play in your communication? How important are visual clues – your expression, your clothes? Now think about your God-conversation. You can't see or (in the normal way of things) hear Him. Is that why some people compensate by gabbling endless words, by drawing attention to themselves through bizarre appearance or by making a loud noise in a public place? Don't they trust that God is there and hears? He isn't deaf. No matter what we do, we can't impress Him. But, unlikely as it seems sometimes, He does love us and He does listen.

I'm struck in this passage by how simple and normal Jesus makes prayer seem. Though God yearns to hear us, He knows what we need before we ask. Like any lover, He appreciates our actions, for example our giving with no ulterior motive. On the other hand, bitterness will poison any relationship. We need to find God's grace to forgive before we can engage in other meaningful conversation with Him.

Jesus doesn't want us babbling the same old words but He does give us a basic pattern for prayer – acknowledging God in His holiness, putting His will first in our requests, then asking Him simply for what we need from day to day. And because each day brings its own challenges, hurts and temptations, He says we need to keep asking for forgiveness – and for help to overcome times of temptation, trouble, and even evil.

Discussion Starters

1. How can our 'covenant behaviour' – the way that we live, give and speak, both within and outside church – show that God is worth everything to us?

2. Can you think of instances where religious hypocrisy has damaged God's reputation?

3. How, and where, do you pray?

4. If you think you weary God with your words sometimes, what could you do differently (Matt. 6:7; 1 Chron. 29:10–20 and Mal. 2:10–3:1)?

5. How is your relationship with God? Do you feel it's all one way – you to Him or Him to you?

6. Do you feel He hears and answers when you pray (see Matt. 7:7–11)? Why not?

_____

_____

_____

7. What can we learn from Luke 11:1–13 and 1 Chronicles 29:11 about how, 'Your will be done on earth as it is in heaven' affects our prayer relationship?

_____

_____

_____

8. What can we learn from Jesus' words and Isaiah 58 about fasting?

_____

_____

_____

9. What are the practical implications in our lives?

_____

_____

_____

10. How does God's grace and forgiveness help us to forgive others?

_____

_____

_____

Personal Application

Remember: 'We do not have a high priest who is unable to sympathise with our weaknesses, but we have one who has been tempted in every way, just as we are – yet was without sin. Let us then approach the throne of grace with confidence, so that we may receive mercy and find grace to help us in our time of need' (Heb. 4:15–16). Before we start doing good deeds, giving, forgiving or praying – before we have any conversation or do anything, we need to know deep in our beings who Jesus is and who we are in Him. We'll then have His grace-gifted confidence to overcome our insecurities, along with the stumbling blocks which they throw up. Do your stumbling blocks include paralysis or acting in your own strength? Seeking wrong control over others or letting others dictate an ungodly agenda?

Seeing Jesus in the Scriptures

Have a look for yourselves, at home. Glance through the Gospels, noting – how did Jesus do 'acts of righteousness'? How did He pray, fast, give and forgive? That's enough Bible skimming to keep you occupied for a week – or, studying in depth, for an exciting year! Be encouraged that Jesus does understand our weaknesses, because He 'emptied Himself' and lived as a human being on this earth. Yet He kept that God-conversation going at all times. That's why the pattern of human/divine relationship He lived out on earth is possible for us to follow.

WEEK 6

Renewed Priorities

Opening Icebreaker and Worship

What is your number one priority in life?

Light a candle. Jesus will be the only light in heaven, His face shining brighter than our sun. For now, fix your eyes on the candlelight – they can bear that. Ask Jesus to show you something of His face, His light as you worship.

Bible Readings

- Matthew 6:19–34
- Psalm 103:13–22
- Hebrews 12:22–29
- Luke 8:21–25
- Matthew 26:36–45

Opening Our Eyes

What are the priorities of your life – with God and with people? Or, to put it another way, 'What are you looking at?' Jesus asks that question in this part of His Sermon.

Television programming seems obsessed with 'makeovers' of house, garden, wardrobe … But what do you notice when you visit someone's house? The value of their furniture and ornaments? Whether their décor and clothes are fashionable? If a corner's left untidy and undusted? Or are you caught up in the warmth of their welcome, the peace (or otherwise) which you find there? Is your main concern with finding out how they are, getting to know them, seeing the image of God within them? Do I sound saintly if I say normally I notice the 'inner' people far more than external things? Yet, when friends are coming for a meal, I worry so much about the externals of cleaning, tidying and cooking that I end up stressed, tired and less able to enjoy their company.

'No, don't look at the kerb, or you'll steer into it. Look at where you want to go!' That's what the instructor said on my first driving lesson. Against my instinct, I had to trust that he was right.

We tend to arrive at whatever we're looking at. There's no merit in living in some squalid tip, just as there's no merit in steering a car into a kerb. Concentrating all our efforts on avoiding those things won't help, though. Better to fix our attention on where we want to go – on God who is the source of everything of value. God knows we don't need the kind of stress which our competitive, materialistic 'makeover' culture leaves in its wake. He also knows that we need clothes, shelter and food – whose exact details of these things are not as important as they appear to us. They are but the contract's 'minor benefits' which run alongside its major provisions and priorities.

If there's one thing I'm really good at, it's worrying. That's why Jesus' words about seeking His kingdom and His righteousness before anything else are key to me. We're hardly living on the brink of starvation and ruin, as were most people Jesus met. But, as that other media obsession keeps reminding us, Doomsday may be nearer than we think. The new breed of terrorists, atomic war, global climate change, unstoppable viruses, to say nothing of the pension crisis looming … the benefits of civilisation could end for us tomorrow. Worry, worry; stress, stress. If we're looking to something other than God for our security, we'll be shaken.

Abraham Maslow, in his famous 'Hierarchy of Needs', said that 'physiological' and 'safety' needs such as air, water, sleep, sex and shelter, must be met before 'higher needs' such as love, fulfilment and one-ness with God. Common sense? It's not what Jesus is saying. And remember He also said the poor, mourning, gentle, hungry, merciful, single-minded, persecuted peacemakers are happy…

Let's spend some time bringing our priorities in line with His this week. Filling our eyes with His light – what more treasure could we want? Fix our eyes on what He wants, make Him boss – and good things follow for the world, not just for us. The reality is that He is boss, He is in charge and He is righteous, faithful and loving. That's the main promise of the deal.

Discussion Starters

1. Where – and what – is your treasure? How much energy do you put into defending it?

2. Light enters the body through the eyes, that's what people of Jesus' time believed. When have you, looking at darkness, become dark yourself?

3. Most of us have to work to live but how can we avoid money and material things becoming our master?

4. How might Jesus' new covenant revoke the curse attached to work in Genesis 3:17–19?

5. Pensions, insurance, home-making, cooking ... What's the line between our own responsibility in these kinds of matters – and God's?

6. What preoccupies and worries you? What does, or might, shake you?

_____

_____

_____

7. What are God's priorities on earth?

_____

_____

_____

8. People in many nations, including Christians, still die as a result of malnutrition or polluted water. What is God's responsibility in this?

_____

_____

_____

And ours?

_____

_____

_____

9. If feeling philosophical, you might like to discuss Maslow's 'Hierarchy of Needs' in relation to this passage.

_____

_____

_____

Personal Application

One good thing about studying the Bible in a group is that we can become accountable to one another. For example, if I say I'm a worrier, people smile and look sympathetic. If I say worrying makes me irritable, robs me of sleep, of peace, of so much energy which I could use for better things; if I say it's a sign of my lack of trust in God, it interferes with His plans for my life, makes me bossy, or apathetic, stops me loving other people as I otherwise might – then I'm confessing sin. When our priorities have become that skewed, as they do sometimes, making ourselves accountable to others can be a real help.

Seeing Jesus in the Scriptures

We can see how Jesus put His words into practice in a situation of real danger, when a terrible storm blew up on Lake Galilee, terrifying all the tough fisherman in the boat with Him (Luke 8:21–25). They were all saved as He spoke the word. We see that same steadfast sense of priority in a starker form as He sets His face to go to Jerusalem (Luke 9:51), in Gethsemane, as He refuses to summon a battalion of angels to rescue Him from the horrors of the cross. His priority was obeying His Father in saving us. Costly, but simple.

WEEK 7

Renewed Foundations

Opening Icebreaker and Worship

Briefly recount examples of things that collapsed because of shaky foundations – a project, relationship, building ...

Sing, read and/or meditate about God as Rock or Jesus as Cornerstone.

Bible Readings

- Matthew 7
- Luke 6:31–33, 41–49
- Isaiah 35:8–10
- John 15:1–11
- Galatians 5:22–23
- 1 Corinthians 3:9–17

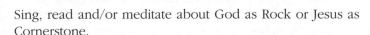

Opening Our Eyes

In a sense the whole Sermon is about foundational matters – certainly last week's study on priorities belongs in this area. Matthew 7 urges us to key three things into our one true foundation – our relationship with the Rock which is Christ:

1. A true understanding of who we are and who other people are, through His eyes.
2. A true understanding of God and His ways – and the danger of people acting in His name falsely.
3. Obeying God and 'doing the stuff'. Merely 'believing' it in our heads won't key us into Christ at all.

Contracts aren't normally renowned for their humour but the first few verses of Matthew 7 could be the script for a knockabout comedy sketch – the kind where you think, 'Ouch! Been there, done that.' Odd, isn't it, that those things which most upset us about others often occur within ourselves? Sometimes they're obvious, sometimes we take care to suppress and hide them.

Verse 6 doesn't seem to fit with the rest of the passage. Jews called Gentiles 'dogs' and 'pigs', so Jesus appears to be telling His Jewish audience not to share the truth about God with non-Jews. He Himself was reluctant to do so as late as Matthew 15:21–28 – but after His resurrection, He told His followers to, 'go and make disciples of all nations' (Matt. 28:19). Maybe then this verse is about God's ways. If we rush ahead of His timing, His Word will be rejected.

Verses 7–11 contain more humour and apply to God-conversations. We're to come to God expecting good (because that's His nature) even though sometimes we have not only to ask, but to seek and knock.

Contracts can often be over-wordy. Isn't it wonderful how Jesus condenses the whole of the Law and the Prophets into one pithy and practical saying in verse 12? It's so much stronger than the more common negative form: 'Don't do to others what you wouldn't want them to do to you.' Echoing His other great summary, 'Love your neighbour as yourself' (Luke 10:27), it's founded on the truth that God loves 'others' as much as He loves me. We are all His children.

Loving God with all your heart, mind, soul and strength is the great relationship foundation expressed here. Jesus uses vivid picture language of the narrow gate and road. It's not an easy option. We have to be single-minded, putting all our efforts into seeking Him and following His ways. His narrow road broadens to a good place – to life in all its fullness. The broad road, on the other hand, narrows as wrongly-founded relationships, lies, jealousy and other sins tend to close down our options and become destructive.

The rest of the chapter has vivid picture language about what happens after being founded, or planted. If we're not firmly founded or planted in God, things will go wrong. If we are, then we need to follow in His ways fully, to obey not just in word but in attitude and deed – in our whole lives. I hope that this series of studies on Jesus' foundational teaching from His great Sermon will help you key into His life, His foundation, His covenant promises and His love.

Discussion Starters

1. Confession time: what annoys you about others that is a fault within yourself?

_____

_____

_____

2. Can you give examples of how God's timing works when bringing His eternal truths to others?

_____

_____

_____

3. How can we be so rooted and grounded in God's love that, even when answers to prayers don't come for a long while, we remain confident that His intentions towards us are good?

_____

_____

_____

4. Consider the practical implications of doing to others what you would have them do to you. What 'others'?

_____

_____

_____

5. What do the narrow gate and road mean in your lives and in the lives of those you love?

_____

_____

_____

6. How can we be sure of bearing good fruit?

_____

_____

_____

7. Do we seek 'signs and wonders' mainly for excitement
or personal blessing?

_____

_____

_____

8. Instead, how can we do the will of God and begin to
see His kingdom come more fully on this earth – to
see 'justice roll on like a river, righteousness like a
never-failing stream!' (Amos 5:24)?

_____

_____

_____

9. What happens to your foundations when a crisis hits?

_____

_____

_____

10. How can we build good foundations into our lives
as individuals, at work, in our wider families and
communities and in our churches?

_____

_____

_____

Personal Application

This is all about humility and going back to basics. About remembering that Jesus' new covenant isn't one which we initiated. It's God's covenant and He sets the terms. He is Lord. He is full of loving-kindness and grace towards us. His demands are simple – frighteningly simple – not to be messed with, but achievable, with His help. He is our Rock. We grow in Him. We grow to be more like Him, to follow His passions. As Jesus said, 'Anyone who has faith in me will do what I have been doing. He will do even greater things than these, because I am going to the Father' (John 14:12).

Seeing Jesus in the Scriptures

The people who normally sat under the authority of their 'teachers of the law' recognised that Jesus' authority went way beyond that. He wasn't presenting a normal kind of sermon or Bible study, quoting the various scriptures and authorities – 'Rabbi X says this but on the other hand Rabbi Y says that.' No, He was speaking God's words and commands in a way that went beyond teaching or prophecy.

People today admire the Sermon on the Mount for its 'high moral teaching' but Jesus was doing far more. He was speaking covenant relationship, directly, as God did to Moses, renewing the foundations of the God/human relationship. The Son of God comes with God's authority, because He is God. He is also fully human here – a unique bridge across which relationship with, and obedience to, God become possible.

Leader's Notes

Material you may find helpful
These books have deepened my understanding of the
Sermon on the Mount.

Matthew for Everyone, Tom Wright, SPCK, 2002.

Matthew, New International Biblical Commentary, Robert
H. Mounce, Hendrickson/Paternoster, 1995.

The Jesus I Never Knew, Philip Yancey, Marshall Pickering,
1995, especially Chapters 6 and 7.

The Powers That Be, Walter Wink, Doubleday, 1998.

Walk On: the spiritual journey of U2, Steve Stockman,
Relevant Books, 2003. I'm fascinated by the way U2's
lyrics resonate with Matthew 5–7, influencing millions
worldwide to oppose kingdom enemies such as poverty
and injustice. I've referred to particular songs which
reflect key aspects of Jesus' Sermon in words accessible
to those with or without church background. Music is
powerful for opening up the imagination, and your group
may find these songs helpful.

Week 1: Renewed Deal

Opening Icebreaker and Worship
If your group is new, you may need to spend time getting
to know each other, perhaps spreading this week's study
over two sessions.

The icebreaker 'agreement' could be a marriage,
mortgage, mobile phone, employment or education

contract ... But don't let questions and answers become too personal or intrusive! It's meant to demonstrate that agreements give responsibilities along with privileges.

Worship places everything in the context of the relationship with Jesus that has to be the foundation of any profitable Bible study.

Break bread and wine simply, having read 1 Corinthians 11:23–26.

Aims of the Session

Before studying the Sermon on the Mount, we're establishing its context within salvation history, particularly in relation to the covenants between God and humankind. We'll find encouragement in the graces offered to help us live by it, in co-operation with Him, until we see His unique rule and authority come on earth as it is in heaven. We'll also be thinking through some of the urgent and honest questions being asked outside of the Church – which we too need to address.

The answers aren't easy. You might like to play U2's *Peace on Earth* from their 2000 album *All That You Can't Leave Behind* (Island). The Northern Ireland peace accords brought real hope after years of conflict, making the loss of many innocent lives in the terrible Omagh bombing which followed even more shocking. The way the song questions God's facile-sounding Christmas-time promise reminds me of a psalmist's honesty in worship. If you want to follow up with something of God's answer, something which, like Jesus' Sermon, turns our 'normal' thinking upside down so that we see from His point of view, try *Grace* from the same album.

Discussion Starters

1. Think personally and globally – from governments through multi-nationals to small employers, for example. In Genesis 2:19–20 God encourages Adam to 'rule' by naming all living creatures. A sermon I heard suggested that we've been misnaming them ever since – calling the elephant 'Source of Ivory', forests 'Dispensable', a fellow human being 'Sexual Object', 'Economic Resource', 'The Enemy' or 'Homeless-Good-for-Nothing'.

2. Everyone in Israel, as well as we in the Church, was/ are meant to be set apart for Him as a light attracting others and demonstrating how to live in right relationship with God and humankind.

7. and 8. You might like to look at Deuteronomy 11:8–32 too – blessings and curses associated with entering the land God promised and with keeping the covenant. It's not easy, we don't gain it all at once! See also Matthew 7:13–14 and Hebrews 8:6–12.

9. We can concentrate so much on certain aspects of how Jesus' sacrifice saves us that we ignore others. I've never heard this one expounded, though parallels with the Passover Lamb, also mentioned in this passage, are frequent. Look up Exodus 20:24 and Hebrews 9:15–18.

Week 2: Renewed People

Opening Icebreaker and Worship

Does happiness, as the word suggests, lie in what happens to us? In what we achieve? Or, as Jesus suggests, does it lie in our inner attitudes – in who we are, in what, and who, are important to us?

Aims of the Session

- To see the deal from God's side by drawing closer to Him.
- To understand Him better – what He likes and dislikes, who He wants us to be.
- To enter more fully into His salvation as a renewed people who can be a light for others.

Notes on the Text

Each week from now on, the main study passage occurs in Matthew 5–7, with any parallel passages in Luke also given. Other Bible readings may illuminate further but, if time is limited, stick with Matthew.

Some pointers to help you with the Beatitudes:

The past and future tenses used in the NIV do follow the original Greek.

V.3: 'poor' means utterly impoverished, destitute, desperate – which reflected the state of many of Jesus' contemporaries. Religious Jews thought the poor were cursed by God, even though their Scriptures constantly stressed His special concern for them. Jesus said He came to preach good news to the poor (Luke 4:18). Luke's Beatitudes omit 'in spirit' – showing that Jesus came for those who are poor in any sense. In fact the materially destitute often turned to Him gladly, while many who believed themselves materially or spiritually rich rejected Him.

V.4: 'those who mourn' may refer to individuals who are bereaved, or to Israel as a nation, mourning freedom and good times with God past. It may refer also to those who share God's grief – mourning as repentance over human alienation from Him, over human cruelty, neglect and the suffering we cause – mourning as repentance. The passage from Isaiah 61 which Jesus read as a manifesto at the start of His ministry (Luke 4) includes 'to comfort all who mourn'. In the New Jerusalem, there will be 'no more death or mourning or crying or pain' (Rev. 21:3–4).

V.5: 'meek' means 'gentle' or 'non-aggressive' and is the word Matthew uses of Jesus entering Jerusalem on a donkey.

V.8: 'pure in heart' would be better translated 'those with undivided heart' or 'the single-minded'. In the Old Testament very few saw God and lived.

V.9: 'peacemakers' is about reconciling.

V.13: in a hot, sweaty climate especially, consuming salt is essential for life – as it was, before refrigeration, for preserving food as well as for bringing out its flavour. When rock salt had all the minerals extracted, the residue was used to prevent people slipping over (rather as our roads are salted today), so it was trampled underfoot.

Vv.14–16: note the city's light is made of a whole community of sources, large and small; the lamp is individual.

Discussion Starters

1. In the West, many churches pay more attention than the Bible does to individuals' relationships with God – and less to that of the community, or society.

4. I've had a go at listing some opposite qualities in the 'Opening Our Eyes' section.

5. Keep this relatively brief.

7. Relationship, growth, grace, obedience …

9. You may well not have time for the last two questions! If you do want to explore this further, look at Exodus 23:25; Deuteronomy 27:26 and Deuteronomy 28.

Resources
Philip Yancey's *The Jesus I Never Knew* has an excellent chapter on the Beatitudes with some great examples of real people.

U2's *I Still Haven't Found What I'm Looking For* (on their albums *The Joshua Tree* and *Best of 1980–1990*) could have been written about the Beatitudes – neither God nor we will have our righteous longings met fully until His kingdom comes.

Week 3: Renewed Morality

Opening Icebreaker and Worship
Tiny examples would be great, rather than something agonised over in prayer for hours. Any relationship affects who we are and therefore what we do. Often subconsciously.

Jesus sometimes appears shows that there is a depth in the Law which goes much deeper than keeping the outward letter, as He does in this week's main passage. I don't always understand His ways – but He is good and He always acts for good, for love.

Aim of the Session
To explore morality in the context of covenant relationship with a holy God who wants – and enables – us to be holy.

Notes on the Text
See this passage in the light of the on-going conflict

between Jesus and the Pharisees, who were forever accusing Him of Law-breaking. Jesus Himself was without sin – and fulfilled every part of the Law as God intended. As St Paul says, don't sin so grace may increase (Rom. 6:1).

V.22: degrees of insult – while *'Raca'* probably meant 'empty headed', 'fool' meant someone who was rebelling against God, acting as though He did not exist.

Vv.24,29: rabbis in Jesus' day often used exaggeration to make their point. Returning to your home in Galilee, to be reconciled with your brother there, required several days journey before leaving your gift at the Jerusalem Temple's altar.

Discussion Starters

3. Remember the various 'old covenants' are not ours. It might help to think in terms of the trivial example of renewing or changing a mobile phone contract – if circumstances have changed, some terms and provisions no longer apply.

8. See Matthew 5:22, Ephesians 4:26–27. I was shocked to learn one Christian woman I know thought of herself as a slut. Clearly, she is anything but. It turned out that her mother had called her that. So had her husband. She needed to be re-named what she was – a woman of God. It took a while for God's truth to erase all the lie-names, but she's there now! Has anyone in the group been called a name which hurt, perhaps causing lasting damage? Has anyone called others names and regretted it afterwards?

9. Take into account cultural differences from Jesus' day. Then, there was no way for a woman to divorce her husband – while a man could simply obtain a written 'bill of divorce' from his wife. Some Jews thought the only ground for divorce was infidelity; others accepted trivial reasons – she'd burnt her husband's dinner or he'd met someone more beautiful. Other scriptures which may be helpful: Matthew 19:3–12; 1 Corinthians 7:39; Proverbs 2:16–17; Deuteronomy 24:1–4. While Jesus must hate the way many today break marriage covenants lightly, in certain circumstances divorce is the lesser of two evils.

10. As I write, just before a parliamentary election, the air-waves buzz with politicians' fervent promises and accusations of lies. Many among the electorate have, from past experience, lost trust in such words. Undecided how to vote, some will abstain, or so the commentators say. That's how lies kill democracy, as they kill trust in relationships. Jesus wasn't speaking about 'swear words' but about vows and oaths. Those aren't so frequent today (apart from legal oaths) but, even in Christian circles, we hear 'yes' when someone means 'no' and vice versa. We hear of lies. We hear of promises, even covenants, broken. The song *Promise* from the Delirious? album *King of Fools* is good on this (Furious? Records).

Week 4: Renewed Justice

Opening Icebreaker and Worship
Do people mention injustices against themselves, loved ones or God's wider concerns?

It might help your thoughts and worship to play U2's *Sunday Bloody Sunday* which is on *U2: War* and *The Best of 1980–1990* – Island Records. Find the words on their website and read them first. The underlying message is that no one will win the Irish or any other conflict through violence. The only good 'battle' is for the kingdom, growing and renewing in this earth the justice, goodness, love, peace and grace which Jesus released on the first Easter Sunday.

Aims of the Session
- To understand intellectually and in action, what God's true justice means in our lives and for our communities.
- To learn to depend on Him as we seek to further His justice and loving righteousness on this earth.

Help people see where they are already fulfilling this practical mission because this is a high-challenge session. It's not something our culture has grasped and so it seems counter-intuitive. It involves sacrifice, and vulnerability. It seems so risky that people need to be strongly established in their identity and trust in Christ. And yet the way we defend ourselves against evil, and stand up for justice, is vital. You might find it helpful to tell the story of *The Three Little Wolves and the Big Bad Pig* by Eugene Trivizas (various publishers and editions). It changes the traditional story just as Jesus forever changed the 'story' of God's relationship with us and ours with each other through His teaching, life, death and resurrection.

Notes on the Text
Matthew 5:38 – compare Exodus 21:23–25: 'If there is serious injury, you are to take life for life, eye for eye, tooth for tooth, hand for hand, foot for foot, burn for burn, wound for wound, bruise for bruise'; Leviticus 24:19–20: 'If anyone injures his neighbour, whatever he has done must be done to him: fracture for fracture, eye for eye, tooth for tooth. As he has injured the other, so he is to be injured'; Deuteronomy 19:21: 'Show no pity: life for life, eye for eye, tooth for tooth, hand for hand, foot for foot.'

Matthew 5:40 – compare Deuteronomy 24:12–13 which says: 'If the man is poor, do not go to sleep with his pledge in your possession. Return his cloak to him by sunset so that he may sleep in it. Then he will thank you, and it will be regarded as a righteous act in the sight of the LORD your God.' And Exodus 22:26–27: 'If you take your neighbour's cloak as a pledge, return it to him by sunset, because his cloak is the only covering he has for his body. What else will he sleep in? When he cries out to me, I will hear, for I am compassionate.'

'Perfect' (Matt. 5:48) means 'complete'. It helps me to think that a tree can be complete and perfect whether it's a tiny sapling or a mighty oak. A baby can be complete and perfect too – but if she were 40 years old and still looked and acted like a baby, something would be incomplete and imperfect – in fact, very wrong.

In Isaiah 42:3 the image is of a damaged reed pipe, coaxed back into musical life by God's gentle hand and breath.

Discussion Starters

6. Where have you heard of, or experienced, Christians making a difference in terms of justice on a local, national or international scale?

Week 5: Renewed God-conversations

Opening Icebreaker and Worship

Keep the icebreaker light-hearted and clear of judgmental attitudes about different 'tastes' in prayer!

Psalm 1 starts us in a good place – acknowledging who God is and who we are in Him. We need to remain in His goodness, grace and love as we face the challenge of Jesus' words in the Sermon on the Mount.

In the Bible, a name represents someone's nature or character. Reflect on how, in the different names of God (Provider, Saviour, Holy One, I am, The Almighty, Healer, Good Shepherd etc) His holiness sits alongside His loving relationship with us.

Aims of the Session
- To renew our God-conversations and covenant behaviour.
- To restore our right relationship with Him and with people.

Notes on the Text
V.1: 'acts of righteousness' comes from the Greek word 'mercies' and, according to Tom Wright, means 'covenant behaviour'.

V.2: a 'hypocrite' was literally a 'play actor' – someone assuming a role or personality which wasn't theirs. It seems that some rich Jews did have trumpets sounded, supposedly to attract poor people to receive alms. Jesus implied that the real motivation was attention-seeking in order to impress other people.

Vv.5–8: The Greek word for 'prayer' literally means 'with a vow' – which takes us back to covenant. Prayer, like fasting, giving and forgiveness, is also 'covenant behaviour'. Pharisees repeated long prayers at fixed hours. Some would ensure they were standing in a prominent place at the appointed times, impressing people with their 'righteousness'. Jews normally stood to pray in synagogues. There's nothing wrong in that – or in sitting, standing, kneeling in church today. Similarly, Jesus repeated prayers, prayed in public and encouraged us to keep making requests to His Father. He is homing in on heart attitude, not physical posture or correct-prayer-form. His Sermon may appear to lay down the law, but we're to read it as relationship, as grace.

V.13: 'temptation' means any trial too difficult for us.
The word used for 'deliver' is strong – 'rescue', 'break our chains'.

V.16: 'fast' means, literally, 'no food'. Jews had four set fasts each year while Pharisees might fast twice weekly. 'Sombre' comes from a word meaning 'like a Scythian' (or Tartar) who were considered sour-faced. Fasting in itself is not what God wants – see Isaiah 58. It needs to be combined with a right attitude towards God and the people He loves – a sharing, in all humility, of His passion and sacrifice on behalf of the poor and oppressed. That is the covenant behaviour which will release God's blessing.

'Jealous God': see Exodus 20:2–12; Malachi 2:10–3:1 and 2 Corinthians 11:2–4.

Discussion Starters

3. There is no one right answer here. For example, it doesn't have to be indoors, or alone. Jesus often prayed in a quiet place outdoors and said, 'Where two or three are gathered in my name ...' (Matt. 18:20). Different people find different ways of praying genuinely helpful: for example silence, tongues, set prayers, quiet meditation using a Bible verse or picture, lighting a candle, playing music, walking while praying, keeping a prayer journal ... What is essential, though?

10. Forgiveness is so important, but don't force things, especially if people are hurting badly. Only God's grace enables us to forgive. We don't have to excuse the person, or pretend no wrong was done. Simply releasing the unforgiven person from our anger and bitterness, into anything good which God has for him/her will release blessing on us too. The contract says that it's up to God to deal with the wrong, if and as He thinks fit.

Try *The Heart of Worship*, either sung or played from Matt Redman's album of the same name.

Week 6: Renewed Priorities

Opening Icebreaker and Worship
It might be good to worship in silence, or perhaps with some quiet instrumental music playing.

Aim of the Session
To re-align our priorities with God's.

If you are finding U2's music helpful, at some point play *Beautiful Day* (on *All That You Can't Leave Behind* and *Best of 1990–2000* albums). It encapsulates much from this session, and is an uplifting song, but takes some understanding, so look at the words first. It helps to know that, when he wrote the song, Bono had recently met a man who had lost everything and was still happy. Also, campaigning with the Christian Aid-initiated 'Jubilee 2000' campaign to relieve Third World debt, Bono was feeling euphoric, having just extracted significant promises from a top financier. In one section of the song there's an almost God's-eye-view from outer space. We see both good and bad in our planet but God still fills it with hope and beauty (there's a reference to the rainbow after Noah's flood). Fix our eyes, our priorities, on God, let go of things which really don't matter – and we will see a beautiful day!

Notes on the Text

This is so familiar. Like me, you may well have studied it before, know it backwards and not find anything in it difficult to understand. But living it ... Well, that's another matter. As you approach it now, try to see through fresh eyes how radical Jesus' words really are.

V.23: Jesus had much to say about spiritual blindness. He also said He'd come to restore sight to the blind – and did so. Philippians 4:8 tells us to think about things that are true, pure, admirable, right etc. Of course, in order to fight evil we have to shine light on it, so we can see it for what it is, rather than pretending it doesn't exist (v.22: 'The eye is the lamp of the body'). But if we normally focus on dark things instead of walking in God's light, then we'll be dark indeed.

V.24: 'Money' appears with an upper case 'M', representing the almost-god of materialism. The old covenant strictly forbids worshipping idols. Trusting in property and money instead of God is idolatry, as well as being foolish.

Vv.28–34: 'Cursed is the ground because of you; through painful toil you will eat of it all the days of your life. It will produce thorns and thistles for you, and you will eat the plants of the field. By the sweat of your brow you will eat your food until you return to the ground' (Gen. 3:17–19). The curse brought by man's rebellion in Genesis was reversed one day a week by Moses' covenant. Under Jesus' new one here, it seems to be revoked for all seven. But have we come into the good of this? Flowers do their 'work' of growing in beauty and setting seed without all the worries and stresses many of us experience.

Discussion Starters

4. Look for practical examples rather than theological niceties. But also discuss why most of us don't fully

enter His 'Sabbath' rest in our lives and work 24/7
– and how we might do so.

9. If you think your group might want to look at
Maslow's 'Hierarchy of Needs', make a note of what
they are first. You'll find the information on the
Internet or in a library (try an encyclopaedia).

Week 7: Renewed Foundations

Opening Icebreaker and Worship
Ask for just two or three examples from the group and
try to draw out the consequences of building on shaky
foundations. Avoid anything too personal, especially in
the church or relationship area, or you could open a
whole can of bitter and poisonous attitudes.

Maybe bring a large stone, or some smaller stones and get
everyone to hold one.

'Cornerstone' – see, for example, 1 Peter 2:6 and Isaiah
28:16. 'Rock' – the many references include Deuteronomy
32:4; 2 Samuel 22:32; Psalm 18:31,46; Isaiah 26:4.

Aim of the Session
To ensure that we are keyed firmly into the Rock – Jesus
– in all that we believe, hope, say and do.

Resource
U2's *Crumbs from your Table* (from their *How to
Dismantle an Atomic Bomb* album) spews out anger at
the kind of Western church which is obsessed with 'signs
and wonders' yet fails to even give their leftovers to those
who are dying in their millions in the developing world.
How can we expect others to believe in our God, in His

care for the poor, in His righteousness, justice and mercy if we don't follow Him in our passion for these same things? If we fail to do so, those who do help, like 'Sister Anne' in the song, who works in a Ugandan hospice, have an almost impossible struggle.

Notes on the Text
Vv.13–14: Isaiah's 'Way of Holiness' may help illuminate this. Do read the whole of Isaiah 35 if you can – for encouragement and vision.

Vv.24–27: the image is of a desert wadi. Normally a dry and sandy valley or depression, if it rains, perhaps miles away, water can rush along it suddenly, sweeping all away in its path. People today are advised never to camp, let alone build a house there!

Discussion Starters
6. John 15 will help you focus on how the life of Christ flows through us to produce fruit. Remaining in His love, and joy, is foundational. Galatians 5:22–23 reminds us what that fruit may be.

9. Paul has some things to say about foundations in 1 Corinthians 3:9–17. Also about the kind of foundations we build into one another – especially when it comes to leaders building the church.

You might like to spend some time assessing what practical and spiritual affects these studies have been having on your group. Building a house that blows down is a waste of everyone's effort. So how can you make Jesus more fully the foundation of all you do and are, together and as individuals? How are relationships – with God, with one another and with the people you meet (or avoid) every day? Has everyone in the group 'bought into' His new deal? Where are people most challenged or shaky still over aspects of His teaching in the Sermon?

On arriving on the scene of a big accident, it's not the ones who scream and shout that worry the paramedics. It's the quiet ones. This is no major-trauma-scene. Nevertheless, pay attention to any who remain quiet in response to your questions about how this teaching is affecting their lives. If silence means that someone isn't feeling challenged by Jesus' words, that's worrying. If someone else is stunned into silence because he or she is overwhelmed by the challenge, you also need to take action. How can you as a group go on helping one another to find God's grace as you move towards doing the 'impossible' – living as fully and righteously as Jesus lived? Pray, with sensitivity, for one another – and on no account avoid asking the group to pray for you, their leader.

National Distributors

UK: (and countries not listed below)
CWR, Waverley Abbey House, Waverley Lane, Farnham, Surrey GU9 8EP.
Tel: (01252) 784700 Outside UK +44 1252 784700

AUSTRALIA: CMC Australasia, PO Box 519, Belmont, Victoria 3216.
Tel: (03) 5241 3288

CANADA: Cook Communications Ministries, PO Box 98, 55 Woodslee Avenue, Paris, Ontario.
Tel: 1800 263 2664

GHANA: Challenge Enterprises of Ghana, PO Box 5723, Accra.
Tel: (021) 222437/223249 Fax: (021) 226227

HONG KONG: Cross Communications Ltd, 1/F, 562A Nathan Road, Kowloon.
Tel: 2780 1188 Fax: 2770 6229

INDIA: Crystal Communications, 10-3-18/4/1, East Marredpalli, Secunderabad – 500026, Andhra Pradesh.
Tel/Fax: (040) 27737145

KENYA: Keswick Books and Gifts Ltd, PO Box 10242, Nairobi.
Tel: (02) 331692/226047 Fax: (02) 728557

MALAYSIA: Salvation Book Centre (M) Sdn Bhd, 23 Jalan SS 2/64, 47300 Petaling Jaya, Selangor.
Tel: (03) 78766411/78766797 Fax: (03) 78757066/78756360

NEW ZEALAND: CMC Australasia, PO Box 36015, Lower Hutt.
Tel: 0800 449 408 Fax: 0800 449 049

NIGERIA: FBFM, Helen Baugh House, 96 St Finbarr's College Road, Akoka, Lagos.
Tel: (01) 7747429/4700218/825775/827264

PHILIPPINES: OMF Literature Inc, 776 Boni Avenue, Mandaluyong City.
Tel: (02) 531 2183 Fax: (02) 531 1960

SINGAPORE: Armour Publishing Pte Ltd, Block 203A Henderson Road,
11–06 Henderson Industrial Park, Singapore 159546.
Tel: 6 276 9976 Fax: 6 276 7564

SOUTH AFRICA: Struik Christian Books, 80 MacKenzie Street, PO Box 1144, Cape Town 8000.
Tel: (021) 462 4360 Fax: (021) 461 3612

SRI LANKA: Christombu Books, 27 Hospital Street, Colombo 1.
Tel: (01) 433142/328909

TANZANIA: CLC Christian Book Centre, PO Box 1384, Mkwepu Street, Dar es Salaam.
Tel/Fax: (022) 2119439

USA: Cook Communications Ministries, PO Box 98, 55 Woodslee Avenue, Paris, Ontario, Canada.
Tel: 1800 263 2664

ZIMBABWE: Word of Life Books (Pvt) Ltd, Christian Media Centre, 8 Aberdeen Road, Avondale, PO Box A480 Avondale, Harare, Zimbabwe, Tel: (04) 333355 or 091301188

For email addresses, visit the CWR website: www.cwr.org.uk
CWR is a registered charity - Number 294387
CWR is a limited company registered in England - Registration Number 1990308.

Day and Residential Courses
Counselling Training
Leadership Development
Biblical Study Courses
Regional Seminars
Ministry to Women
Daily Devotionals
Books and Videos
Conference Centre

Trusted all Over the World

CWR HAS GAINED A WORLDWIDE reputation as a centre of excellence for Bible-based training and resources. From our headquarters at Waverley Abbey House, Farnham, England, we have been serving God's people for 40 years with a vision to help apply God's Word to everyday life and relationships. The daily devotional *Every Day with Jesus* is read by nearly a million people in more than 150 countries, and our unique courses in biblical studies and pastoral care are respected all over the world. Waverley Abbey House provides a conference centre in a tranquil setting.

For free brochures on our seminars and courses, conference facilities, or a catalogue of CWR resources, please contact us at the following address.
CWR, Waverley Abbey House, Waverley Lane, Farnham, Surrey GU9 8EP, UK

Telephone: +44 (0)1252 784700
Email: mail@cwr.org.uk
Website: www.cwr.org.uk

CWR CRUSADE FOR WORLD REVIVAL
Applying God's Word to everyday life and relationships

Further new titles in the fast-growing *Cover to Cover* series

Proverbs
Living a life of wisdom
Ruth Valerio
ISBN: 1-85345-373-0

1 Corinthians
Growing a Spirit-filled church
Christine Platt
ISBN: 1-85345-374-9

Fruit of the Spirit
Growing more like Jesus
Selwyn Hughes with Ian Sewter
ISBN: 1-85345-375-7

Jeremiah
The passionate prophet
John Houghton
ISBN: 1-85345-372-2

Ecclesiastes
Hard questions and spiritual answers
Christopher Brearley
ISBN: 1-85345-371-4

£3.99 each (plus p&p)
(Prices correct at time of printing)

Other titles in this series

Hosea
The love that never fails
*Selwyn Hughes
with Ian Sewter*
ISBN: 1-85345-290-4

James
Faith in action
Trevor J. Partridge
ISBN: 1-85345-293-9

God's Rescue Plan
Finding God's fingerprints
on human history
Catherine Butcher
ISBN: 1-85345-294-7

1 Timothy
Healthy churches –
effective Christians
Chrisine Platt
ISBN: 1-85345-291-2

The Divine Blueprint
God's extraordinary power
in ordinary lives
Gary Pritchard
ISBN: 1-85345-292-0

John's Gospel
Exploring the seven
miraculous signs
Keith Hacking
ISBN: 1-85345-295-5

Moses
Face to face with God
Elizabeth Rundle
ISBN: 1-85345-336-6

2 Timothy and Titus
Vital Christianity
Christine Platt
ISBN: 1-85345-338-2

Rivers of Justice
Responding to God's call to
righteousness today
Ruth Valerio
ISBN: 1-85345-339-0

Nehemiah
Principles for life
*Selwyn Hughes
with Ian Sewter*
ISBN: 1-85345-335-8

Hebrews
Jesus – simply the best
John Houghton
ISBN: 1-85345-337-4

Parables
Communicating God
on earth
Chris Leonard
ISBN: 1-85345-340-4

£3.99 each (plus p&p)
(Prices correct at time of printing)

The Kingdom
Studies from Matthew's Gospel
Chris Leonard

ISBN: 1-85345-251-3

The Image of God
His attributes and character
Trevor J. Partridge

ISBN: 1-85345-228-9

The Letter to the Romans
Good news for everyone
John Houghton

ISBN: 1-85345-250-5

The Tabernacle
Entering God's presence
Ian Sewter

ISBN: 1-85345-230-0

The Covenants
God's promises and their relevance today
John Houghton

ISBN: 1-85345-255-6

The Uniqueness of our Faith
What makes Christianity distinctive?
Selwyn Hughes with Ian Sewter

ISBN: 1-85345-232-7

Joseph
The power of forgiveness and reconciliation
Elizabeth Rundle

ISBN: 1-85345-252-1

Ruth
Loving kindness in action
Elizabeth Rundle

ISBN: 1-85345-231-9

Great Prayers of the Bible
Applying them to our lives today
Jennifer Oldroyd

ISBN: 1-85345-253-X

Mark
Life as it is meant to be lived
Christine Platt

ISBN: 1-85345-233-5

The Holy Spirit
Understanding and experiencing Him
Selwyn Hughes with Ian Sewter

ISBN: 1-85345-254-8

Ephesians
Claiming your inheritance
Trevor J. Partridge

ISBN: 1-85345-229-7

£3.99 each (plus p&p)
(Prices correct at time of printing)